W9-ANM-506

art of japan

art of japan

wood-block color prints

BY CAROL FINLEY

Ⳑ LERNER PUBLICATIONS COMPANY ■ MINNEAPOLIS

Copyright © 1998 by Carol Finley

Website address: www.lernerbooks.com

Library of Congress Cataloging-in-Publication Data

Finley Carol.
    Art of Japan : woodblock color prints / Carol Finley.
      p.   cm. — (Art around the world)
    Includes bibliographical references and index.
    Summary: Focuses on Japanese wood-block prints of the Edo period
    (1600–1868) by explaining the subject matter as well as the
    technique used in making them.
      ISBN 0-8225-2077-X (alk. paper)
      1. Color prints, Japanese—Edo period, 1600–1869—Juvenile
    literature. 2. Ukiyoe—Juvenile literature. [1. Prints, Japanese.
    2. Painting, Japanese.] I. Title. II. Series.
    NE1321.8.F5 1998
    769.952—dc21   97-28421

Manufactured in the United States of America
1 2 3 4 5 6 – JR – 03 02 01 00 99 98

Contents

Introduction

A **Japanese print is a picture printed on** paper from carved blocks of wood. The most famous Japanese prints were produced from the 1600s to the late 1800s. But Japanese printmaking especially flourished between 1750 and 1850 in the city of Edo—present-day Tokyo.

The wood-block print of the Edo period (1600–1868) is called a *ukiyo-e* print. Ukiyo-e is a word of Buddhist origin that means, "pictures of the floating world," or "scenes of transitory importance." These prints were not considered to be formal art. They were the art of the merchant class—as opposed to the "official" art of the high-ranking shogun and the samurai. Ukiyo-e prints were light-hearted celebrations of the passing scene, and they provided a glimpse of Japanese people's everyday life, their cultural activities, and the natural beauty of their country. In other words, the prints present a portrait of life in Japan at that time.

Japan was then a closed country. In 1603, a man named Ieyasu became shogun. His family, the Tokugawas, ruled Japan for more than 250 years. The Tokugawa government believed that contact with the outside world must end to maintain order within the country.

Wood-block prints from the Edo period showed scenes from everyday life. Here, a man chases his hat, which the wind keeps just ahead of him. *Riverscene,* Ando Hiroshige

The scene below is meant to give a sense of the prosperity of the city of Edo. Swallows flit through a summer sky streaked with bright yellow, while a stylish young woman, the bold patterns of her dress a mark of the late Edo taste, passes along the nearby ferry landing. In the middle of the river, an oarsman sculls his small boat, leaving a deep blue wake that suggests swift movement. Beyond him to the right a cargo boat is laden with boxes marked "tea." To the left of the print is the prow of a large cargo ship that hauled much of the trade that supplied Edo.

Both prints are by Ando Hiroshige (1797-1858). *Hibiya and Soto-Sakurada, left. Yoroi Ferry, Kaomi-Cho, below.*

The impressive building that stretches along the far side of the moat, *above,* is one of the most detailed depictions of a daimyo mansion found in any ukiyo-e print. The elaborate design of the gate shows that the residence belongs to a person of high rank.

In the print to the right, a ferry loaded with a standing crowd can be seen in the distance. The viewer looks westward at the harmonious regularity of the many warehouses, where commodities such as rice, soy, and oil—brought in from all parts of Japan to supply the shogun's capital—were stored.

A daimyo travels with his impressive entourage. Note the figures balancing a tufted standard in the cups of their hands. From time to time, they engaged in displays that involved twirling and tossing the standards in the air. This print, *Nihon Bridge, Yedo View,* is also by Ando Hiroshige.

People stroll past shops in a typical *Street Scene* by Katsushika Hokusai.

During the 1630s, Japan cut its ties with other nations and isolated itself from the rest of the world. The Japanese were not permitted to travel outside of Japan, and foreigners, with few exceptions, were not permitted entry into Japan.

The country had a formal social structure with different classes of people. A person's status was determined by the class into which he or she was born.

The shogun, or chief military commander, ruled the country from his compound in Edo. In 1800, Edo was one of the largest cities in the world, with a population of about one million residents. The emperor, who was primarily a ceremonial figure, lived in the capital, the ancient city of Kyoto.

Under the emperor and shogun were the daimyo—feudal lords who ruled the provinces. The daimyo pledged absolute loyalty to the shogun. To insure their loyalty—to insure against revolts led by the daimyo—these feudal lords were required to leave their families in Edo, under the jurisdiction of the shogun, whenever they were in the provinces.

Under the daimyo were the samurai warriors, who were trained in combat arts. The samurai made up the armies of the shogun and the daimyo, and they were highly respected on the social scale. Farmers and artisans occupied the lower end.

Merchants were at the very bottom of the social scale, but they had the benefit of economic prosperity. This was a time of economic growth in Edo, and the merchants, who provided the goods and services to the other residents, benefited tremendously. The wood-block print grew in popularity because the merchants patronized the artists and promoted their prints. These prints provide a vivid picture of Japanese life during the 1700s and 1800s.

Chapter one

How
Prints
Were
Made

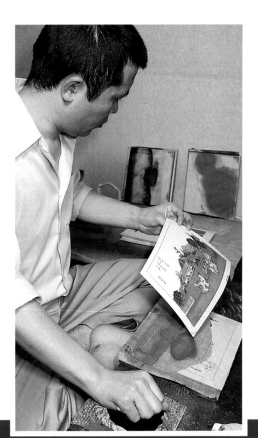

This artist demonstrates the complete printmaking process.

JAPANESE PRINTS DEVELOPED FROM ILLUSTRATIONS in popular books. Many people became interested in the pictures themselves, so publishers began to produce the illustrations separately. The early prints were made in black and white, although the artists sometimes added other colors by hand. Around 1750, artists pioneered a new technique to create multicolored prints, which became extremely popular.

The technique of making prints involved many highly skilled artisans in addition to the artist who made the original design. This group effort was coordinated by the publisher. The publisher commissioned the artists, hired carvers and printers, and arranged for the sale of the finished prints.

Black-and-white prints were made from one block of wood. First, the artist made a design for the print with brush and ink on paper. The carver then attached the paper to a block of wood. This artisan carved out the design on the wood by carefully cutting away all the wood between the lines of the drawing, which left only the design itself raised. All the lines had to be very precise. Next, a printer applied ink to the raised surface of the woodblock and placed a piece of paper on top of the block. The printer rubbed the back of the paper with a smooth pad. When he or she pulled the paper from the block of wood, the design appeared in print.

The production of color prints required many blocks of wood, usually one for each color. The carver cut each block so that the only areas left raised were those to be used for the

same color. The blocks were keyed with markings so the different areas of design all lined up. The printer then applied various colors to the blocks and placed the paper on each block in succession—one after the other. The end result was a multicolored print.

A print might use 12 woodblocks, and since a block could be used many times, a few hundred or even a thousand prints might be made from them. *Print Studio* (**figure 1**) by Utagawa Kunisada (1785–1864) shows artisans making prints. In the right-hand panel,

Figure 1
Print Studio
Utagawa Kunisada

one artist is making a design with brush and ink on paper. The woman beneath her is sharpening the wood-carving tools. Wood blocks are stacked under the window. The wood-carver, at the top of the center panel, is carving a design into a block of wood. The woman in the blue-and-white head scarf is wetting the paper for printing. The remaining woman and the two women in the left-hand panel assist in hanging the paper to dry. Bowls of colored ink and pads for printing are also seen in the left-hand panel.

Figure 2
Store Selling Picture Books and Ukiyo-e
Katsushika Hokusai

When the prints were finished, they were
sold in a local shop. A print by Katsushika
Hokusai (1760–1849), *Store Selling Picture
Books and Ukiyo-e* (**figure 2**), shows such a
shop. This print was hand colored with ink
rather than colored with separate wood
blocks. It resembles the prints that were made
before the invention of the multicolored
wood-block print. Compare it to Kunisada's
Print Studio (**figure 1**) to see the difference in
technique.

In Hokusai's print, a samurai—the man
with two swords hanging at his side—and
other customers are looking at the offerings in
a print shop. The prints are stacked in piles,
and if you look closely, you can see some of
the designs. The sign in front identifies the
store as belonging to Tsutaya Jusaburo, a well-
known print publisher whose trademark was a
three-peaked mountain over an ivy leaf.

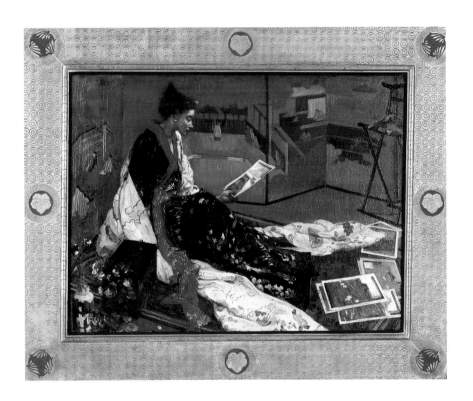

Caprice in Purple and Gold, No. 2—The Golden Screen, James A. M. Whistler, 1871. Japanese prints had a powerful impact on the style of Whistler. In this painting, the diagonal line of the screen leads the eye to the central figure of the lady. She is dressed in a Japanese kimono and is surrounded by rich, colorful materials and artifacts from the East. Her attention is centered on a Japanese wood-block print, one of many scattered around her.

Wood-block prints were produced in large quantities and sold cheaply in ordinary shops such as the one illustrated. Ordinary Japanese people were the main buyers of the prints. The prints were thought of in the same way that you might think of a poster or a postcard.

Ukiyo-e prints made their way to Europe after Japan opened its borders to the outside world in the late 1850s. Japan then began trade with Western nations. In Europe, decorative items from Japan became very fashionable. Japanese prints were first noticed by artists who appreciated their aesthetic merit. Edouard Manet, Claude Monet, James McNeill Whistler, and Vincent van Gogh were among the group of painters who admired the prints and adopted some of the design principles and motifs into their own work. Because of this, ukiyo-e prints were influential in the development of Western art. Their monetary value did not increase until the late 19th century, when collectors—particularly in Europe—began to buy them. They are now displayed in the major museums of the world.

Japonaiserie: The Bridge in the Rain, Vincent van Gogh, 1887.
Van Gogh was influenced by Japanese prints. He based this painting on a wood-block print by Ando Hiroshige. See how similar it is to the Hiroshige print on page 31.

Chapter two

Subjects
of
Ukiyo-e
Prints

WOOD-BLOCK PRINTS WERE MADE FOR THE ordinary citizen, and this dictated the choice of the subject matter. The main subjects included landscapes; bird and flower pictures; portraits of beautiful women—often geisha or courtesans; theater scenes and portraits of actors; sumo wrestlers in competition; and scenes of everyday activities. Although many people were involved in making a single print, the artist who designed it was the pivotal figure.

The Landscape Print

The Japanese have had a long tradition of appreciating nature. They celebrated the changing seasons, the new moon, and the appearance of cherry blossoms in spring. Some ukiyo-e artists were landscape specialists. The two most important artists who worked in this area were Katsushika Hokusai (1760–1849) and Ando Hiroshige (1797–1858). Between them they brought the landscape print to a new level of achievement.

Katsushika Hokusai was a strong-willed individualist. In his long career he produced art for more than 70 years. He did sketching, painting, and book illustrating, as well as designing for wood-block prints.

In the city of Edo, an artist usually began a career by working as an apprentice in the studio of an established artist, and most artists retained this affiliation. Hokusai was first apprenticed to a book illustrator and then to the studio of Katsukawa

In the spring, Japanese people gather to admire the beautiful cherry blossoms, *top*. Flowers are an integral part of Japanese life. The Japanese have made decorative arrangements of cut flowers since the sixth century. In traditional kimonos, a mother and daughter practice this art, called *ikebana*.

Figure 3. *The Great Wave off Kanagawa*
Katsushika Hokusai

Shunshō, where he designed *kabuki* theatrical
prints. Kabuki is a form of Japanese drama
that developed in the 1600s.

Sometime after 1793, when Shunshō died,
Hokusai was either thrown out of the studio
or he left on his own accord. He moved
around to different studios and worked on his
own. He worked on diverse subjects, including portraits of women, sumo wrestlers, birds
and flowers, and landscapes. During his career
Hokusai adopted many pseudonyms—ficti-
tious names—the most famous being "the old
man mad with painting."

Hokusai was an artist with a flair for the
dramatic. In *The Great Wave off Kanagawa*
(figure 3), Hokusai has shown the contrast
between the great power of nature and the
insignificant power of humans. In this action scene, a gigantic wave is poised to
come down on two boats. The oarsmen in
each boat are temporarily holding their
boats steady. When the wave hits, it seems
they will be overcome with water and may
capsize. The wave is the focal point of this
print. Viewers have to look carefully to
even see the boats. The power of the wave

is immense, and the boatmen appear to be at the mercy of nature. Even majestic Mount Fuji, seen in the background, looks small by comparison.

Sometimes artists do a series of prints on one subject. *The Great Wave off Kanagawa* is from a series called "The 36 Views of Mount Fuji." There are, in fact, 46 prints in this series. Hokusai added 10 prints to the original 36 because of the great success of the initial designs. Each of the prints shows Mount Fuji, Japan's highest mountain, from a different vantage point, and with a different scene surrounding it.

Mount Fuji at Dawn, or *The Red Fuji* (**figure 4**), is another print from the same series. In this print, the snowcapped mountain is the main subject. Fuji, which is an inactive volcano on the outskirts of Tokyo, is colorfully depicted. Hokusai shows the quiet strength

Figure 4. *Mount Fuji at Dawn,* or *The Red Fuji,* Katsushika Hokusai

High-speed bullet trains have become a symbol of Japan's efficient railway system. They can travel 150 miles per hour. Mount Fuji stands in the background.

and permanence of the mountain and the tree line below, contrasted with a blue sky filled with white clouds.

These two prints, perhaps Hokusai's two most famous works, emphasize drama and power by focusing on a single element of nature. Most of the other prints in the series show Mount Fuji from afar.

Many Hokusai prints provide glimpses of daily life. Travelers are carrying bundles and baskets of food, some travelers are resting in a tea house, workers are building houses, oxen are carrying loads, and farmers are working in fields. Mount Fuji, a familiar landmark, is the ever present background. Is there a noteworthy feature in your town or city that would make a good subject for a series of prints?

Ando Hiroshige was another eminent landscape artist. He achieved fame when he completed a series called, "Views of the 53 Stations of the Tōkaidō." The Tōkaidō was the road that connected Edo to Kyoto, the imperial capital. Many dignitaries, tradesmen, and other travelers went back and forth between these two major cities for business and pleasure. Most travelers covered the distance —over 300 miles—on foot. The journey, when walked, took about two weeks. For the convenience of travelers, 53 stations, or rest stops, were situated along the way. Visitors could find food, drink, and lodging at each station. In more modern times, travelers can take a high-speed bullet train along the Tōkaidō instead of walking.

In 1832, Hiroshige accompanied an official government party traveling the Tōkaidō. Along the way, he made sketches of each station. These sketches became the basis for his series. Among the prints are scenes showing travelers making their way along the road, porters carrying baggage, walkers resting at an inn, and horses in a field. This series was enormously popular when it was first printed.

Collectors bought prints of their favorite portion of the road or they bought the entire series. It established Hiroshige's reputation as a major artist.

Shinagawa: Sunrise **(figure 5)** portrays the first station a traveler encountered after leaving Edo. This part of the journey along the Tōkaidō follows the coast of the Pacific Ocean. Sailing ships can be seen in the water.

Figure 5. *Shinagawa: Sunrise,* Ando Hiroshige

Figure 6. *Ohashi: Sudden Shower over Atake*
Ando Hiroshige

Travelers carrying their loads are making their way down the road, while a few on the right are taking a break. Across from them, three women attendants stand at a tea house. Viewed together, the prints in this series provide a visual record of the Tōkaidō journey.

Hiroshige had a great interest in weather and liked to depict people braving the elements. One of his best-known prints is *Ohashi: Sudden Shower over Atake* (**figure 6**). This print is from a series Hiroshige did on views of Edo. Six walkers and one raftsman are suddenly caught in a downpour. They struggle to hold their own and attempt to shield themselves as best they can from the rain. Black clouds fill the upper sky, and the rain obscures the buildings across the river. Hiroshige used long broad lines to represent the falling rain. This print captivated artists in Europe. In 1887, Vincent van Gogh made a painting called *The Bridge in the Rain* that was directly inspired by Hiroshige's woodblock print. (See page 22.)

Colorful fireworks illuminate the sky over the Sumida River in modern Tokyo.

Fireworks—a popular evening diversion for the people of Edo—were frequently shot off for festivals and holidays. Hiroshige's *Ryogoku Bridge: The Fireworks* (**figure 7**) shows the night sky glowing with a burst of fireworks. Spectators watch from the bridge and from the boats below. Hiroshige achieves a beautiful contrast between the midnight blue sky and the fiery explosions beneath it.

Hiroshige had worked in an artist's studio from the age of 14, but his father was a fireman, and Hiroshige inherited this post from him. When his own son came of age, Hiroshige gave him the post and then devoted the rest of his own life to art. He went

両国
川びらき
玄火

東都名所

Figure 7. *Ryogoku Bridge: The Fireworks*, Ando Hiroshige

Figure 8
Stork and Bamboo
Isoda Koryusai

on to raise landscape prints to a position of great popularity in Edo. Hokusai and Hiroshige were the most successful ukiyo-e landscape artists.

Bird and Flower Prints

Bird and flower subjects derive from a form of traditional painting that originated in China, and ukiyo-e artists made use of those subjects. Prints of this type are called *kacho-ga*. In addition to images of birds and flowers, ukiyo-e artists also illustrated animals, insects, and plants. Instead of the grand views of nature found in landscape prints, kacho-ga prints are small studies of a single feature of nature.

Sometimes the beautiful prints were published in books that featured a whole series of birds, flowers, insects, or animals.

Isoda Koryusai (dates uncertain) was the first ukiyo-e artist to work extensively in the kacho-ga category. He was a samurai who gave up his rank to become an artist. Koryusai, at first a follower of Suzuki Harunobu, emerged as a major printmaker in the 1760s and 1770s. *Stork and Bamboo* (**figure 8**) is an example of a kacho-ga print. A single stork stands on one foot and twists its neck to look at a large bamboo plant that is next to him. A patch of irises blooms in the background. This elegant composition celebrates the beauty and meditative quality of nature.

Kabuki plays, melodramatic representations of historical or domestic events, are still performed in modern-day Japan.

Kabuki Theater

Theater is a major form of entertainment in Japan. Kabuki is a form of traditional Japanese drama developed during the late 1600s. It combines dramatic action, dance, pantomime, and music to tell a story. The actors dress in colorful, elaborate costumes, wear striking makeup, and use an exaggerated acting style. During the Edo period, a night at the theater meant witnessing a larger-than-life spectacle rather than a portrayal of a realistic event. A narrator often filled in details of the story by chanting or singing. All parts were played by men because the government forbade women from performing in kabuki. The government also regulated the number of theaters allowed. There were three in Edo.

Kabuki plays were melodramatic portrayals of historic or domestic events. Kabuki actors enjoyed enormous popularity with the public. Usually born into theatrical families, they studied acting from childhood. People often came to see a particular actor and his unique interpretation of his role in the play.

Many ukiyo-e artists made prints of actors in their most famous roles. Tōshūsai Sharaku (dates uncertain) was an artist who specialized in prints of actors. Almost nothing is known about Sharaku's life except that he

Figure 9
*The Actors Bandō Zenji as Oni Sadobō
and Sawmura Yodogorō as Kawatsura Hōgen*
Tōshūsai Sharaku

worked producing prints during a 10-month period between May 1794 and February 1795. After that, details of his life are a mystery.

Sharaku made over one hundred prints that convey the dramatic, exaggerated style of kabuki acting. His print *The Actors Bandō Zenji as Oni Sadobō and Sawmura Yodogorō as Kawatsura Hōgen* **(figure 9)** shows the portraits of two actors during a performance of *Yoshitsune Sembonzakura*. The taller figure is Kawatsura Hōgen, a good character who gives shelter to Yoshitsune while he is in flight from his brother, who wants to have him killed. The figure with the shaved head is Oni Sadobō, an evil priest who is interested in Yoshitsune's downfall. The contrast of good and evil is one of Sharaku's favorite themes. Especially interesting is the way the two hands—one clenched in a fist, the other with fingers spread wide—are used to give the picture an extra sense of life.

The faces of the actors are highly expressive. Sharaku was able to capture the nature of the character portrayed by the actor. Colorful costumes and striking makeup added to the spectacular dramatic effect.

Kabuki actors wore a crest on their kimonos. The crest identified the actor with his family of origin. The actor on the right has a circular crest with a design in it. The crest of the actor on the left is a square with a crane. Crests might be made of various geometric shapes, waves, or other patterns. Crests were worn by other Japanese as well, including samurai who also used them to mark their possessions.

Okumura Masanobu was a leading early ukiyo-e artist, who was also a publisher and bookseller. He produced hand-colored prints and some made with two colors. Masanobu originated several technical advances during his long and productive career. The subjects he chose to depict include portraits of women and scenes of kabuki theatre.

The Nakamura Theater, Edo 1740 (**figure 10**) is a two-color print of Masanobu's that shows a kabuki play being performed in a theater. The main actor in the center of the stage is sharpening an arrow. A large audience watches from the central pit and from two levels of wood-enclosed sections. Lanterns

Figure 10
The Nakamura Theater, Edo 1740
Okumura Masanobu

with different crests hang from the rafters. Peddlers walk through the audience selling food and drink. This print captures the atmosphere of a kabuki performance. The two principal actors are both elaborately dressed.

Members of a kabuki audience were forbidden backstage—but to see something of the actor's life behind the scenes, a fan might buy a print. *Otani Hiroju III in the Dressing Room* **(figure 11)** was made by Katsukawa Shunshō (1729–1792), one of the major artists who portrayed kabuki actors and an influential teacher to a generation of printmakers, including Hokusai. Shunshō often portrayed actors in relaxed surroundings. In this print, Hiroju sits cross-legged on the floor as he paints his face in front of a mirror. The mirror sits on a small chest were he keeps his theatrical makeup. Next to him is a younger man, and behind him stands an actor dressed to play a woman's role. In the background, you can see some of the necessary possessions for an actor, such as a box of assorted kimonos and a bundle holding swords that the actor used when portraying a samurai.

Figure 11. *Otani Hiroju III in the Dressing Room*
Katsukawa Shunshō

By looking at the kabuki prints, you can get an impression of this kind of theater. The kabuki play still remains popular in Japan, but people also enjoy new dramas by Japanese and Western playwrights.

Portraits of Women

Portraits of women were another major focus of ukiyo-e prints. The clothing, hairstyles, features, and demeanor of women were all important factors. Women were shown dressed in fine kimonos, often made of multi-layered, patterned silk. They tied these colorful robes with a large sash called an *obi*. Often these women were famous geisha or courtesans. Geisha were trained from childhood in the arts of conversation, dance, and music.

Suzuki Harunobu's depictions of graceful young women in tranquil surroundings established his reputation as one of the masters of the Japanese wood-block print. *Woman Admiring Plum Blossoms at Night* **(figure 12)** is a characteristic Harunobu portrait. He shows a young, delicate woman in a tranquil scene. In this print, the woman holds a lantern while standing on a balcony at night. She looks up at the tree's white blossoms, which stand out against the black, night sky. The woman is wearing a beautiful, striped kimono patterned

Figure 12. *Woman Admiring Plum Blossoms at Night*
Suzuki Harunobu

Figure 13
Geisha with Samisen
Utagawa Kuniyasi

with birds. Harunobu was famous for the delicate quality of the women in his prints. He is credited with being one of the originators of the multicolored print.

Geisha with Samisen **(figure 13)** by Utagawa Kuniyasi (circa 1800–1880) shows a woman in layers of an elaborate, decorative kimono. Waves, birds, and flowers decorate this garment. The woman's hair is styled with ornaments, and she holds a three-stringed musical instrument called a samisen. During the Edo period, wood-block prints revealed the latest fashions the way fashion magazines show popular clothing styles in more modern times.

An age-old Japanese form of wrestling, called sumo, draws huge crowds. This photo shows the entering ceremony of upper level wrestlers wearing silk and gold ceremonial aprons.

Sumo Wrestling

The national sport of *sumo*, a Japanese style of wrestling, dates back centuries, and it is still a major spectator sport in Japan. Athletes compete by using the strength of their entire body to overcome the opponent or to force him out of the ring. Rigorous training involves developing mental and spiritual discipline as well as physical strength.

Massive body size is a characteristic of sumo wrestlers. There are no weight restrictions or weight classes as in Western fighting sports. In sumo, a wrestler with enormous body size can have the advantage. The match takes place in an elevated ring, and usually many matches involving different wrestlers are held in a single day.

In sumo, the contestants engage in a series of ritual body exercises before the physical contact begins. First, each wrestler stamps his feet in his corner of the ring. He raises each leg as high as possible and brings it down with the greatest force he can muster. This represents the stamping out of the opponent. The wrestlers drink from individual bowls of water and then sprinkle salt into the center of the ring. The salt is symbolic of purification.

When the match begins, the contestants face each other in a squatting position, rub their hands together and hold their arms out. More foot stamping takes place before the wrestling begins. The preliminary movements create tension between the opponents, prepare them psychologically for combat, and engage the attention of the audience.

The fight takes only one round and is often over in seconds. The winner is the man who causes his opponent to step out of the ring, even for an instant. Also, if either man touches any part of his body to the ground, other than the feet, he automatically loses.

Here, the wrestlers are shown in one of the preliminary rituals performed before the match begins.

44

Two Sumo Wrestlers of the Eastern Group: Nijigadake Somaemon and Fudenoumi Kinemon **(figure 14)** by Katsukawa Shunshō is a print of two famous sumo wrestlers. Both men have the characteristic massive bodies with broad shoulders and large biceps, the large, flexible muscle of the upper arm. Even their feet are enormous. The wrestler on the right looks older and more tired and worn out. Shunshō, the artist of this print, also made one of the kabuki prints in this book. (See **figure 11** on page 39.)

Figure 14
Two Sumo Wrestlers of the Eastern Group: Nijigadake Somaemon and Fudenoumi Kinemon, c. 1782
Katsukawa Shunshō

Another print by Shunshō shows a sumo match in progress. *Match between Fudenoumi and Miyagino* **(figure 15)** shows two huge men, each struggling to overcome the other. A referee watches intently from behind them. Other wrestlers, waiting their turn in the ring, sit and watch from the front rows. The stands are filled with spectators. The wrestlers, shown larger than life size, are fighting under a four-posted Shinto shrine—the traditional setting for a wrestling match until the 1950s, when the posts obstructed television cameras. In this print, Shunshō has captured the drama and excitement of sumo wrestling.

Most wrestlers were supported by samurai or daimyo. The wrestlers competed in annual festivals and special tournaments. These events lasted for 10 days at a time in open areas of the city. Some of the money raised went to local temples and charities. Sumo wrestlers adopted special fighting names, and

Figure 15
Match between Fudenoumi and Miyagino
Katsukawa Shunshō

many had large followings. These fans made up the market for the sumo prints.

Each print had to appeal to as many fans as possible. Since no devoted fan would buy a print showing his hero going down to defeat, it was important that all fight scenes be neutral, as the ones shown here are. For similar reasons, the faces of both contestants had to be equally visible.

Children

Ukiyo-e artists also designed pictures of the children of Edo. The prints show a range of activities from work to play. Torii Kiyonaga (1752–1815) was a major figure of the ukiyo-e art world in the 1780s. He established his reputation by doing prints of beautiful women in an elegant style. Kiyonaga's print *Minamoto Shigeyuki Executing Calligraphy* **(figure 16)** shows a six-year-old child prodigy who is a master calligrapher. In a shop, in the company of a woman who may be his mother and a man who may be the shop's owner, the little boy demonstrates his mastery of this difficult art form. Great skill and dexterity are necessary to make beautiful calligraphy. A brush and ink are used to write the graceful characters. The tools of the calligrapher are shown on the floor, surrounding the boy and on the chest behind him. Some examples of his writing are displayed around the shop and in the open drawers of the chest. Calligraphy was a high art form, and examples of beautiful work would be displayed in the same way as a prized painting.

Figure 17
Boy Water Vendor
Suzuki Harunobu

In *Boy Water Vendor* (**figure 17**) by Suzuki Harunobu, a small boy balances a pole with two buckets of water on his shoulder. On the front bucket is a tray and cup for serving tea. Children of Edo sometimes worked from an early age at menial jobs in the fields, shops, and streets.

The print *Catching Fireflies* (**figure 18**) by Eishosai Choki (circa 1785–1805) shows a leisure activity. In this print, a woman and child are strolling along a brook at evening. The child tries to capture a firefly. The woman looks on, holding a small cage ready for any fireflies the child may catch.

The artist, Choki, is known for his images of ideal female beauty. Women of graceful elegance are characteristic of his work. The woman in this print is beautiful and refined. The pattern on her kimono mirrors the shape of the fireflies that light the sky. Vivid flowers decorate her obi. A field of beautiful irises makes up the background of this print. This print combines landscape and figures in a captivating way.

Figure 18
Catching Fireflies
Eishosai Choki

Some scenes from modern-day Tokyo

Conclusion

UKIYO-E PRINTS ENJOYED A GREAT POPULARITY IN Edo during the 18th and 19th centuries. Viewers can still look at them to learn about kabuki theatre or sumo wrestling or to admire the fashions popular during that period. Japanese printmakers were masters of portraying the human figure and the Japanese landscape. The prints of the Edo period are a beautiful and fascinating form of art. We can appreciate them for their aesthetic value and also for what they tell us about the everyday life of the Japanese people during that period.

For Further Reading

Japan in Pictures, (Minneapolis: Lerner
　　Publications Company, 1994).

Selected Bibliography

Hillier, Jack. Japanese *Masters of the Colour
　　Print*. London: Phaidon Press, 1954.

Lane, Richard. *Images from the Floating
　　World: The Japanese Print*. New York:
　　1978.

Link, Howard A. *The Theatrical Prints of the
　　Torii Masters*. Honolulu: Honolulu
　　Academy of the Arts, 1977.

Michener, James A. *The Floating World*.
　　Honolulu: University of Hawaii Press,
　　1954.

Munsterberg, Hugo. *The Japanese Print*. New
　　York: Weatherhill, Inc., 1991.

Stewart, Basil. *A Guide to Japanese Prints and
　　Their Subject Matter*. New York: Dover
　　Publications, Inc., 1979.

Index

Colophon

Art of Japan: wood-block color prints was composed by Interface Graphics, Inc., in the Goudy typeface with display lines in Gill Sans, printed by the John Roberts Company on 80-pound Patina Matte, and bound by Muscle Bound Bindery, Inc., in Minneapolis, Minnesota.

About the Author

Carol Finley studied art history at Northwestern University and did graduate work at Bryn Mawr College. She worked as a trader in the financial markets before pursuing a career in writing. She lives in London and New York City.

Photo Acknowledgments

Amsterdam, Van Gogh Museum (Vincent van Gogh Foundation), 22; (Tsutaya:Edo, Kyowa 2.1802), plate 46, #761.952H7A, photograph © 1997 The Art Institute of Chicago, All Rights Reserved, 20; (image 26x19.7 cm), purchased from Frederick S. Colburn, Kate S. Buckingham Fund, Clarence Buckingham Collection of Japanese Prints, 1952.356, photograph by Greg Williams © 1998, The Art Institute of Chicago, All Rights Reserved, 35; (image 46.3x67.9 cm), Clarence Buckingham Collection, 1925.2285, photograph © The Art Institute of Chicago, All Rights Reserved, 38; (image 25.8x38.8 cm{Oban}), Frederick W. Gookin Collection, 1939.707, photograph © 1997 The Art Institute of Chicago, All Rights Reserved, 39; (image 26x38.2 cm), Frederick W. Gookin Collection, 1949.44, photograph © 1997 The Art Institute of Chicago, All Rights Reserved, 44; Gift of Miss Katherine S. Buckingham to the Clarence Buckingham Collection, 1925.2027, photograph by Greg Williams © 1998, The Art Institute of Chicago, All Rights Reserved, 48; Art Resource, NY, 26–27, 28; Bettmann Archive, 8–9; © The British Museum, 49; Brooklyn Museum of Art Collection, 11 (both); Photo by P.J. Buklarewicz, 50–51 (bottom right); Cameramann International, Ltd., 16 (all), 24 (both), 42, 43, 50 (left top and bottom); Corbis-Bettmann, 7 (detail), 13; Courtesy of the Freer Gallery of Art, Smithsonian Institution, Washington, D.C., (Accession no. 04.75), 21; Giraudon/Art Resource, NY/Musee des Beaux-Arts, Angers, France, 30, 31, 53; Courtesy of the Arthur M. Sackler Museum, Harvard University Art Museums, Gift of the Friends of Arthur B. Duel, 23 (detail), 45; Japan National Tourist Organization, 29, 36; Metropolitan Museum of Art, Fletcher Fund, 1929 (JP 1506), Photograph © 1994 The Metropolitan Museum of Art, 40; Metropolitan Museum of Art, Harris Brisbane Dick Fund and Rogers Fund, 1949 (JP3115), photograph © 1994, The Metropolitan Museum of Art, 2, 37; The Newark Museum/Art Resource, NY, 12, 32–33; Philadelphia Museum of Art, Given by Mrs. John D. Rockefeller, 5 (detail), 47; UPI/Corbis-Bettmann, 32 (upper left); Victoria & Albert Museum, London/Art Resource, NY, 15 (detail), 18–19, 41.

Front cover: The Victoria and Albert Museum, London/Art Resource, NY
Back cover: Art Resource, NY